Puffy

people whose hair defies gravity

by Aya de León

Please see page 21 for photo credits.

To order this book please visit:
http://puffyhairproject.wordpress.com.

Dedication

To puffy-haired people

   everywhere

Our hair is like a dancer

It leaps up and

   defies gravity

**Puffy bush. Puffy tree.
Both are puffy. Just like me!**

4

Puffy here.
Puffy there.

Yay!
I love my
puffy hair.

Puffy thick. Puffy round.
Puffy in a sparkly crown.

**Puffy here.
Puffy there.**

**Yay!
I love my
puffy hair.**

Puffy curl. Puffy kink.
Puffy twirl to help me think.

**Puffy here.
Puffy there.**

**Yay!
I love my
puffy hair.**

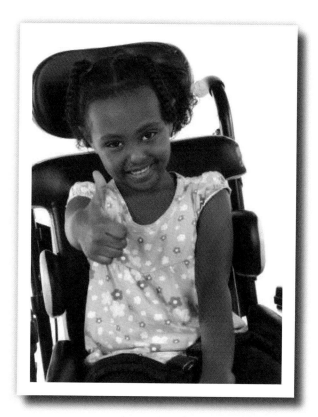

9

Puffy here. Puffy there.
Puffy, puffy everywhere!

Puffy love.
Puffy care.

Yay!
I love my
puffy hair.

**Puffy inside.
Puffy out.**

**Puffy dancing
all about.**

**Puffy here.
Puffy there.**

**Yay!
I love my
puffy hair.**

13

Puffy one. Puffy two.
Puffy playing peek-a-boo.

**Puffy here.
Puffy there.**

**Yay!
I love my
puffy hair.**

Puffy settles soft and light against my pillow every night.

Puffy here.
Puffy there.

Yay!
I love my
puffy hair.

Acknowledgements

Special thanks to all the individuals and families who submitted photos, the Failure Club at HackerMoms, Jess Clarke at Red Star Black Rose Digital Production Services, Anna de Leon, Stuart McCalla, my own puffy hair girl D, Denene at MyBrownBaby.com, Michelle at Mutha Magazine, Vanessa VanDyke, Tiana Parker & all the other young puffy hair warriors out there.

Photo Credits

Front cover photo licensed from Shutterstock.

Back cover photo, Vanessa VanDyke.

Yvonne Fly Onakeme Etaghene (p. 6, upper left) by An Xiao.

Coco Peila (p. 8, upper right) by Shauna Hundeby.

Katsi Santamaria (p. 14, upper left).

Women Hugging (p. 15, top) licensed from Getty Images.

Girl with Thumbs Up (p. 15, bottom) licensed from Getty Images.

Sleeping Child (p. 16, top right) licensed from iStock images.

Sleeping Mother and Baby (p. 16 bottom) licensed from Shutterstock.

All other images used with permission of maker.

Aya de León

About the author

Beneath the giant pink foam afro wig, children's book author Aya de León is a writer/performer for adults working in poetry, fiction, and hip hop theater. Her work has received acclaim in the *Village Voice, Washington Post, SF Chronicle, SF Bay Guardian, American Theatre Magazine*, and has been featured on Def Poetry, in *Essence* Magazine, and various anthologies and journals. She is currently working on a sexy feminist heist novel. Aya is the Director of June Jordan's Poetry for the People program, teaching poetry, spoken word, and hip hop at UC Berkeley.

For more info on Aya de León:
http://ayadeleon.wordpress.com
or on twitter @ayadeleon.

For more info on The Puffy Hair Project:
http://puffyhairproject.wordpress.com.